THE

GHOSTLY TALES

OF

CHATTANOOGA

Published by Arcadia Children's Books
A Division of Arcadia Publishing
Charleston, SC
www.arcadiapublishing.com

Spooky America is a trademark of Arcadia Publishing, Inc.

First published 2021

ISBN: 978-1-5402-4937-1

Library of Congress Control Number: 2021938352

Notice: The information in this book is true and complete to the best of our knowledge. It is offered without guarantee on the part of the author or Arcadia Publishing. The author and Arcadia Publishing disclaim all liability in connection with the use of this book.

All images courtesy of Shutterstock.com; p. 35 Bob Pool/Shutterstock.com; p.102 Kenneth Sponsler/Shutterstock.com.

Spooky America

THE GHOSTLY TALES OF CHATTANOOGA

AMY PETULLA
AND JESSICA PENOT

Adapted from *Haunted Chattanooga* by Jessica Penot and Amy Petulla

arcadia
CHILDREN'S BOOKS

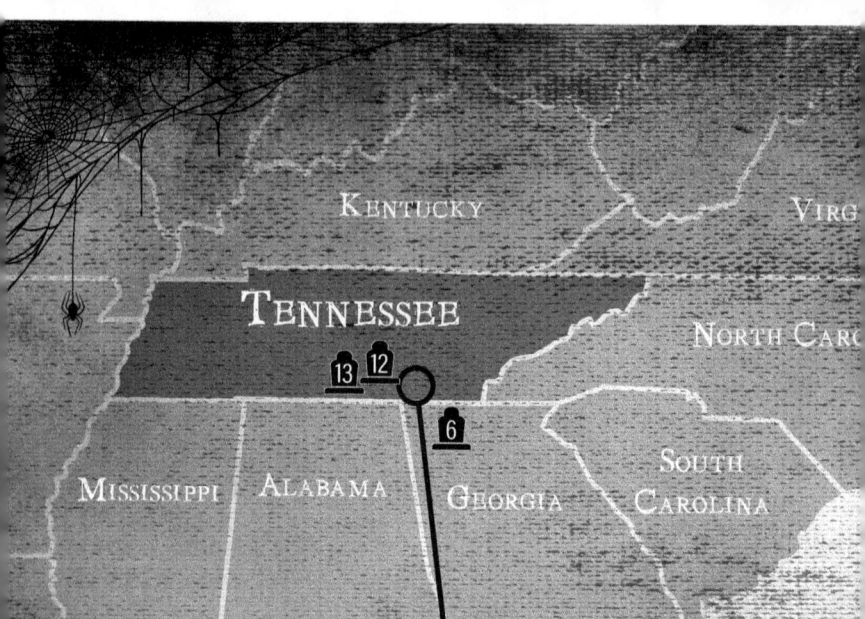

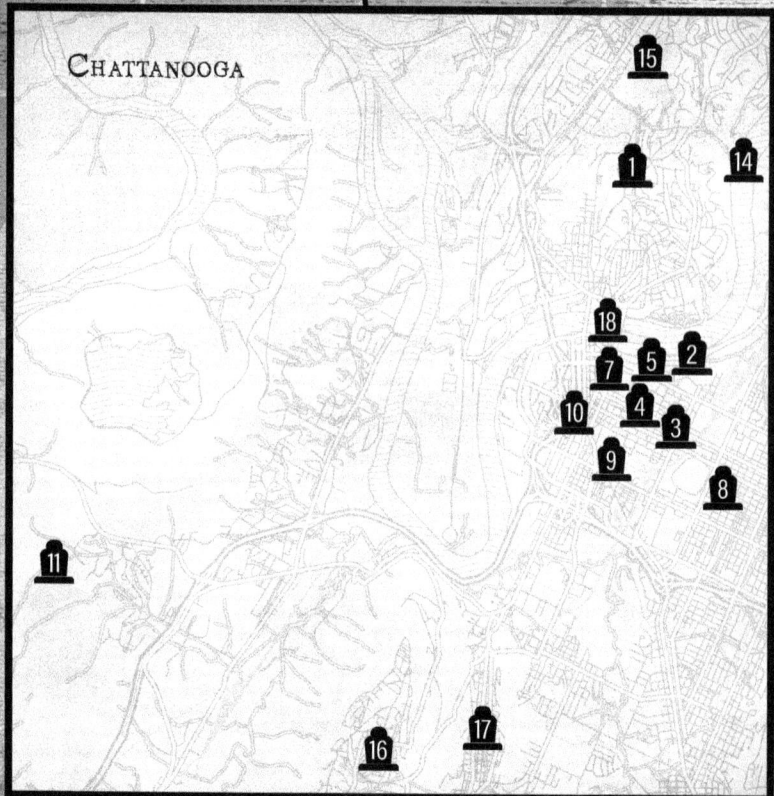

TABLE OF CONTENTS & MAP KEY

Walnut Street Bridge

Introduction

Welcome, fearless readers! Come explore the spooky side of Chattanooga. Nicknamed the "Scenic City," it is known for what it has to offer for daytime. Sure, there are mountains, caves, and rivers, as well as museums and historical sites. But what about the unseen world that likes to come out to play at night?

The city has a storied past full of ghosts and legendary creatures. While some doubters would scoff, there are so many reports of mysterious happenings that even the city library has a huge file of newspaper reports of them! And they are getting bolder. Not only do they sometimes peek out of photos, once in a while, they even speak!

The ghosts of Chattanooga can be found all around. From caves and rivers to schools and jails, the shadow world is DYING to scare you with the real spirit(s) of the town. After all, our history is jam-packed with historical tragedies, murders, villainy, and heroism that keep these ghosts hanging out here. The Civil War, the Trail of Tears, and a school that made its students bring their own dead bodies for class all helped shape the city's life and afterlife. So it is no surprise that ghosts can be found around every corner. Some are sad, some are confused, and some are downright angry, but they are all fun to hear about!

So turn on all of the lights and check under the bed before curling up with the covers pulled tight—a night filled with the spirits of southeast Tennessee lies ahead.

School Spirits and Grave Situations

Ghosts LOVE schools. It's probably because they remember the fun they had there. And Chattanooga's oldest high school, Chattanooga High, is no exception. The school has had six locations, and the last two have been haunted! Since 1998, Chattanooga High has been located in the North Shore neighborhood and has been known as the Center for Creative Arts (CCA). (In that year, it became a magnet school, and students have to audition to get in.) Unsurprisingly, the ghost there is associated with its performance arts space. From 1922 to 1964, Chattanooga High was located in the Third Street building, which now houses Chattanooga School for the Arts and Sciences (CSAS), and there were multiple ghosts haunting that space. But those are not the only haunted schools in Chattanooga.

Just a block away from CSAS is the University of Tennessee at Chattanooga (UTC), which also has its share of ghosts. And what do you think lies between these two "spirited" schools, tying the area together into the ultimate home for ghosts? Four—count 'em, four!—graveyards on a single lot! The Paupers Cemetery is an unmarked field where the bodies of the poor and unknown were buried. Early city residents are decomposing in Citizens Cemetery. The Jewish Cemetery is the only one of the four cemeteries still accepting new occupants. And the Confederate Cemetery obviously holds lots of Confederate soldiers from the Civil War. But it is also the last resting place of at least two Union soldiers.

In the ghost hunts that happen there every weekend, ghost-hunting equipment goes crazy around these Union graves, and many full-body apparitions have been captured in photographs there. Perhaps this is because the Confederate soldiers are trying to chase away the enemy from their resting grounds. But the activity around the Union tombs is not the only surprise. The latest resident of the Confederate Cemetery was found more than a century after the war. In 2000, builders who were putting in a swimming pool on Missionary Ridge got quite a shock when then uncovered the remains

of a long-dead soldier. He was moved to the Confederate Cemetery—a much better resting place than a swimming pool.

Citizens Cemetery is also full of ghostly activity. One ghost who says his name is Tim hangs out near the front of the grounds and often chats through the talking piece of ghost-hunting equipment called the Ovilus. He gives his name, flirts with ghost-hunting guests, and sometimes even tells his story of being hanged from a tree there.

But the Paupers Cemetery is home to the most restless ghosts. Why? Nearly all of their

unmarked graves were plundered for body parts by students at the former UTC Medical School. Can you believe they had to get their own cadavers (dead bodies used for dissection) for class?! Even a county official in charge of the graveyard was caught robbing the graves in November 1894 to sell the corpses that were not rotting too badly to out-of-town doctors. So as you can imagine, those unhappy ghosts are still stalking the grounds, seeking their bodies, and creating bursts of electromagnetic activity in the process.

UTC's most famous ghosts are the bride who is said to have committed suicide in an

on-campus church known as Patten Chapel after being left at the altar and a groundskeeper named John Hockings, who killed himself in Hooper Hall. John Hockings's story is well documented. In 1974, he died by inhaling gas in the chemistry lab. Ever since, people often report hearing footsteps when no one is there, feeling an unseen presence breeze by, and experiencing a cold chill right before he sends the elevator up or down, with no living person pressing the buttons.

The bride, who is known as Anna, is not shy about making herself known. How do we know her name? She has given that name dozens of times through the Ovilus equipment in the Shakespeare Garden behind the chapel. She frequently says bad things about men, and when brides-to-be visit, she warns them about getting married! Anna also often asks for coffee, and guests have smelled coffee many times when she is present. She even sometimes appears in photos!

At CSAS, the third-floor library is home to the spirit of Colonel Creed Bates, who was principal of Chattanooga High for thirty-six years. In 2010, a previous custodian told me he often felt a presence there late at night. Although the temperature was normal in the library earlier in the evening, when he returned to turn off the lights, he would feel a cold chill in a particular spot the principal used to like. Sometimes he would return there after turning off the lights only to find "something" had flicked them on again. Do you think Colonel Bates wants the lights on because he is trying to read in the library?

The former custodian also heard children's laughter coming from a second-floor classroom at night, when no children could

possibly be present. The sound continued as he approached the room. He put his hand on the knob and slowly opened the door, only to find—nothing! No kids, no adults, no iPod playing, no windows rattling, nothing to cause the sound. He checked to see if someone might have hidden or snuck out, but no one was there—at least, no one living! And he is not the only one to experience a spirit there. Others have reported actually seeing a ghost in the second-floor hall.

The last ghost reported at CSAS was in the gymnasium. As the story goes, you can still hear someone dribbling a basketball in the gym late at night, long after everyone else has gone home. Some people believe it is the pro basketball player Anthony Jerome Roberts, who played for the Denver Nuggets and Washington Bullets. He went to school there and sadly died young. Perhaps he returned after death to a place he was happiest in life.

While CSAS is still on Third Street, Chattanooga High School (now CCA) is on the other side of the river. The school only has one ghost, but he is one of my favorites! Even before it became an arts school, that building had a grand auditorium with a full orchestra pit. However, that kind of space has its risks. No student suffered a major injury from a tumble off the brink. But according to legend, one custodian was not so lucky. In the late 1970s,

"Old Joe," as he is known, fell backward off the stage into the pit and died. The school decided to close up the pit. However, one student's father told me how he and other parents snuck in to tear the boards off after it became an arts school. They seem to have let Joe's spirit out when they did so.

Joe is heard, felt, and smelled in a couple of places. When he worked there, the custodians used to hang out near the assistant principal's office and smoke. A strong smell of cigarette smoke wafts through there when Joe is around. As you might guess though, his favorite haunt is the auditorium stage. Many students hear footsteps across the stage and see the curtains moving when no one is up there. One student told me that she saw the curtains open by themselves, and she and others heard a sound like a janitor's bucket being rolled across the stage. It seems old Joe is glad the pit was reopened so he could resume his old "life." Would you be brave enough to audition for a play if you had to share the stage with a ghost?

Civil War Cannon at Chickamauga Battlefield

CHAPTER 2

Chilling Chickamauga

According to the legends that surround it, Chickamauga has always been a dark and haunted place. It is believed that many of the indigenous Cherokee contracted and died from smallpox when settlers came to the area. Some people say that Chickamauga means "the river of death" in the Cherokee language—a name that speaks to the tragedy that surrounds the place. This may be just a legend, but the place is haunted by more than legends.

Today, Chickamauga National Military Park is a pretty and peaceful place that sits just south of Chattanooga. Cannons used in battle, as well as monuments and plaques dedicated to soldiers who died here, are dotted across the beautiful stretch of grass. Families come to explore the site and enjoy picnics on the soft, green grass.

However, during the Civil War, this place was anything but pretty and peaceful. The Battle of Chickamauga took place here in September 1863 and was the largest Union defeat of the Civil War. With 16,170 Union and 18,454 Confederate casualties, the Battle of Chickamauga was the second

costliest battle of the Civil War, ranking only behind Gettysburg. Due to the number of fallen soldiers, it took months to clean up the battlefield. People came looking for their loved ones, their husbands and sons, their fathers and brothers. They carried lanterns as they wandered through the battle site, hoping to find their soldier.

To this day, those who visit Chickamauga say they can hear the weeping and see the light from the lanterns of those searching for their loved ones. They also claim to hear phantom horses and strange cries in the night. Some visitors even say they have seen ghostly soldiers wandering the field. And a local legend describes a female ghost who wanders the battlefield at night looking for her lost fiancé.

Chickamauga seems to be under a curse, as the Civil War battle isn't the only reason that the place is known for sadness and tragedy.

After the Civil War, the location became a training site for soldiers going to fight in the Spanish-American War. Although the camp was not there long, disease and death tore through it. Supposedly, many soldiers committed suicide while stationed there. Death seems to have become Chickamauga's constant friend.

However, it isn't the ghosts of the dead that hold the most interest for paranormal explorers of this battlefield. It is a cryptid called Old Green Eyes. (A cryptid is an animal, such as Sasquatch or the Loch Ness Monster, that has been claimed to exist but never proven to exist.) The origins of Old Green Eyes are unknown, and most believe he is an ancient monster that has been wandering the fields of Chickamauga as long as there have been fields there.

It is believed that all the death and suffering that took place at Chickamauga drew him to the place. Wherever Old Green Eyes comes from, people describe him as looking like a human with huge green eyes, a massive and hideous jaw, and horrible fangs. Stories about him say that he has run cars off the road and caused people to run into traffic.

The best description of Old Green Eyes comes from a park ranger named Edward Timney. During an interview, he described walking through the park in the middle of the night when a chill rushed over his body. The next moment, Old Green Eyes was almost on top of him. Timney said, "When it passed me, I could see his hair was long like a woman's. The eyes—I'll never forget those eyes—they were glaring, almost greenish orange in color, flashing like some sort of wild animal. The teeth were long and pointed like fangs. I did not know whether to run or scream or what. Then the headlights of an approaching car

came blazing through the fog, and the thing disappeared right in front of me."

The park isn't open at night, so you don't have to worry about seeing ghosts, hearing phantom horses, or running into Old Green Eyes in the dark. But that's not to say that you won't experience all of that during a visit in the daytime ...

CHAPTER 3

Ghostly Gallows

Back in the 1800s, Chattanooga had two jails: Swaim Jail, named after John Swaim, the horrible man who kept this jail in his home, and the Hamilton County Jail. And both jails were said to be haunted by the men who had been imprisoned and died there.

During the Civil War, James Andrews, a civilian, came up with the plan to defeat the South by hijacking one of their supply trains, burning bridges, and tearing up tracks along the way. Several Union soldiers and a couple of other men signed on to help. On April 12, 1862, Andrews's Raiders, as they came to be known, stole the *General* locomotive from Kennesaw, Georgia, while the conductor, W.A. Fuller, was having breakfast nearby. When he saw his engine pulling out without him, he tried at first to chase it on foot. He and his crew eventually switched to a train to chase down the train thieves. Just before reaching Chattanooga, the Raiders' vehicle ran out of fuel, and they all jumped off and scattered. A search with bloodhounds led to the capture of Andrews and his accomplices, and they were taken to "the hole," a tiny, dark, stinking, rat-infested, burning-hot dungeon under the trapdoor of Swaim's jail. The men were packed in so tightly that if one of them turned, the whole row of men had to turn. On top of that, they had no way to wash and only an open bucket for a toilet. So as you can imagine, the stench was unbearable. Peee-ewww!

Andrews and several other Raiders were hanged for their crime. They were later declared heroes.

This tragic event gave rise to two separate ghost stories. One claims that two shadows are seen darting around the area where the jail once stood. People have heard footsteps when no one else is around and have taken ghost photos at that spot. When I attempted to take a picture of the location in 2011, I jumped and nearly dropped my camera when the image on the screen revealed a tall, menacing green figure. As I glanced up from the camera, I saw nothing, but the phantom was there every time I glanced back at my equipment. When I finally

snapped the photo, the figure was replaced by a large sunburst. Though it has never shown up again, I still tell myself the huge acid-colored apparition was just glare!

The more unique ghost is at the graveyard where Andrews's Raiders are all buried. The story goes that, during certain full moons, the train monument actually leaves its pedestal and chugs through the hills of the cemetery. The pedestal is left empty, and a soft moaning, like the chuffing of a train engine, can be heard echoing through the trees. You may think this is unbelievable, but reports of ghost rail cars are more common than you might guess. They say that Abraham Lincoln's funeral train appears each year on the anniversary of its mournful trip!

The other local outlaw haunt is the old Hamilton County Jail downtown. When Buddie Wooten and George Knapp robbed a saloon in

1895, they were tried, found guilty, and like the Raiders, sentenced to hang. But before they were hanged, Buddie threatened Sheriff Hyde that he would come back to haunt him. They were hanged together, but Buddie was the last to die.

At that time, the rumor in the jail was that the ghost of whoever was last executed was allowed to return to visit the site of his death until the next condemned man died there. It's said that Buddie Wooten regularly used that as an escape from his otherwise burning afterlife below. For nine years after his death, no other hangings took place, and Buddie would appear around the gallows. He would moan, groan, and let out strangled gasps before finally disappearing. Once in a while, Buddie would even help out the guards by scaring the daylights out of a particularly difficult prisoner.

One prisoner in particular was worse than all the others. Piggie Jones screamed, pounded the walls, and stirred up all the other prisoners, even after being hosed down and left all night in a freezing cold, pitch-black cell. However, suddenly one night, his cell near the gallows became quiet as a tomb. Piggie then started promising to be good if they would only PLEASE get him out of that cell. Apparently, Buddie had put the fear of God into that Piggie.

Even though the old jail was torn down in 1976 and replaced, people continue to get orb photos outside the building. Ghost hunters call the round white balls of light sometimes seen in photos "orbs" and say it is a ghost trying to appear. Is it just a bit glare or dust floating through the air, or could Buddie still be hanging around? No one knows. Are you brave enough to visit and find out?

The Chattanooga Choo Choo

Boo at the Choo Choo

The legendary Chattanooga Choo Choo is the city's most iconic attraction. The train running to the city was given the nickname in 1880. And the Chattanooga Choo Choo was the subject of the very first-ever gold record! These days, however, "Chattanooga Choo Choo" refers to the hotel and entertainment complex that occupies the station built for the train in 1908.

Most of the people enjoying the rooms, restaurants, escape room, and other attractions in the complex don't know that they are sharing space with some unseen guests. If you looked up while in the former Gardens Restaurant, you might wonder why there was a card stuck to the ceiling with a knife. One night in the late 1970s, a traveling magician named Mr. Lucky told a crowd at the restaurant that it was his last show. For his very last trick, he threw the five of diamonds high in the air with one hand, tossed a knife with the other, and impaled the card to the ceiling. And what do you think happened next? He went home and died that very night, of course! But the trick was more impressive than anyone knew at the time. Why? Because workers at the restaurant were NEVER able to get that card down from the ceiling! Every time they tried, something bizarre happened. For example, when one employee climbed a ladder to remove it, he reached out to grab a pipe for balance, and even though it had been cool a moment before, it instantly became burning hot. Employees decided Mr. Lucky's ghost wanted evidence of his last trick to remain there forever, so they left it. The card remained in that spot for more than forty years, until the entire ceiling was torn out during a remodel in 2019. I'd say that was pretty lucky, wouldn't you?

Mr. Lucky is not the only person who has left something behind. The African American porter whose photo hung near those of Franklin and Eleanor Roosevelt in the former model train lobby (now Songbirds Guitar Museum) still haunts the hotel long after his death. He still tries to assist with guests' luggage, though they are a little scared when it is moved by an unseen hand! He is also sometimes seen outside the Victorian railcars, where you can stay for the night. His other post-death stomping ground is out near the train tracks, where he swings a signal light. Do you think he might be trying to prevent the horrible train wreck that left the station with its other ghost?

Another ghost is a mother looking for her child. She is my favorite ghost of the Chattanooga Choo Choo, though her story is tragic. She is usually seen on the walkway right above the entrance doors to the lobby atrium. Why would she hover there? Because right underneath are old train schedule signs, and the trains named below her are the *Royal Palm* and the *Ponce de Leon*. The fateful wreck

of these two trains left her at the Choo Choo for eternity, searching for her child.

Two days before Christmas in 1926, the *Royal Palm* left Chattanooga headed for Atlanta, while the *Ponce de Leon* passed through Atlanta heading to Chattanooga and then Chicago. Rain was falling so hard you could barely see. In nearby Rockmart, the *Ponce de Leon* was supposed to take a side track so the two trains could pass. However, it was coming down a steep hill, going way too fast. It missed the switch, and the two trains crashed head-on. Investigators found out later that the engineer, a man named S.J. Keith, had let a road foreman hitching a ride drive

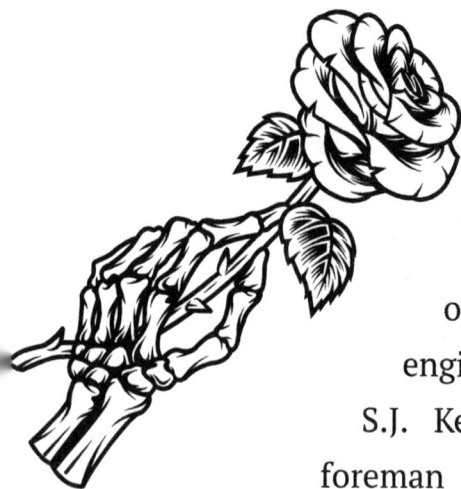

the train while he went to rest in the passenger car. Twenty people died on the *Ponce de Leon*, including a little girl named Goldie. Her mother, Elsie, was badly hurt but survived the crash. I think Elsie continues to linger at the station so that she can check the train schedules, hoping that one of the trains will bring her daughter back. What do YOU think?

Ghosts Who Refuse to Check Out

Read House, a hotel in downtown Chattanooga, is a charming and inviting building. It is surrounded by lovely trees and looks like a quiet place to stay while visiting Chattanooga. You might think it was a good place to start a wonderful vacation.

But Read House has a dark history that most people do not know about. Read House was originally built as an inn, called Crutchfield

House, in 1847 by a man named Thomas Crutchfield. The inn was built right across from the new railroad station so people traveling would have a convenient and comfortable place to stay. For a while, it was one of the most successful hotels around—but everything changed in 1861.

That year, Jefferson Davis, who would be elected president of the Confederate States of America, visited Crutchfield House and spoke of his plans for the southern states to succeed from the Union. Thomas Crutchfield supported the Union, and he got terribly angry when he heard Davis's plans. Punches were

thrown, guns were drawn, and the shooting started. Bloodshed was prevented only because Crutchfield's son dragged him from the room. Crutchfield sold the hotel soon after this.

When Union forces took Chattanooga in November 1863, Crutchfield House became a hospital for Union soldiers. The place became a witness to the pain and death of the nearby battlefield. Many soldiers who had been wounded in battle died of their injuries in the hospital. What was once a cozy inn immediately became soaked in the blood of the Civil War. And it would seem that more than a few of those soldiers decided to stay

around and continue to defend the place in the afterlife.

The hotel burned down in 1867. A man named John T. Read saw hope in the ashes of the old hotel, and he bought and rebuilt it. The new hotel was beautiful, and it would have been easy to forget all the ghosts that once roamed the old Crutchfield House. But the ghosts never slept, and neither did history. The long shadows of all the people that had died in the Crutchfield stayed to remind people of what had happened before.

The most famous ghost of Read House is a young woman named Annalisa Netherly, who was supposedly murdered in Room 311 at the Crutchfield House by a young Union soldier. Despite her death, Annalisa did not leave the hotel. If you ask the staff of the Read House about the ghosts that haunt this place, they will always tell stories about Annalisa. They believe she is responsible for unexplained noises, flickering lights, faucets turning on and off, shadowy figures, and more. It is claimed that if a smoker goes into Room 311, Annalisa becomes so furious that she starts throwing things around the room.

In my visit to Room 311, I did not see anything of Annalisa. It was quiet, and the guests staying in the room seemed happy. But perhaps Anna was just taking a day off or the guests hadn't done anything to upset her—yet. If you get a chance to stay at the Read House, will you be brave enough to ask to stay in Room 311?

Raccoon Mountain Caverns

Smoking Can Be Hazardous to Your Afterlife

For most people, falling asleep on the job might lead to, at worst, being fired. But for Willie Cowan, the night watchman at Raccoon Mountain Caverns, the result was much worse. His punishment for falling asleep with a cigar in his hand was an eternity on duty—without pay.

Locals and tourists alike love visiting Raccoon Mountain Caverns. When it first opened to the public in 1931, the fun was just the cave itself. But, in its heyday, several rides were added. In 1966, a tram was installed that took visitors to a Native American village at the top of a mountain. In 1979, they added go-karts, a water slide, horseback riding, panning for gems, a very scary alpine slide, and at one point, even a hang glider on a rope!

But the cave has always been the main attraction. "Officially discovered" in 1929 by Leo Lambert, some people say that it was local boys who actually first found the cave. On the western side of U-shaped Raccoon Mountain, farmers spent long hot days working in the fields on land owned by the Grand Hotel, located in downtown Chattanooga. The farmers needed a way to cool off in the stifling heat of southern summers. They found that cool air

blew from cracks in some of the rocks, and that boulder pile became a favorite spot to rest and relax. The men wondered if the breezes might come from a cave beneath the mountain, but it was some of the farmers' sons who discovered the truth. Bored from waiting for their dads to finish work, they went in search of mischief and found a promising gap only a foot wide in the rocks. They wriggled their way through the child-sized passage until they were rewarded with the discovery of a large chamber.

The boys' fantastic stories of what lay beneath the mountain finally prompted the adults to invite Leo Lambert, who had recently discovered nearby Ruby Falls Cave, to see if he might find a cavern here, too. He had to squeeze through a small crack and crawl through the mud crevice. Covered in dirt, he found a cave he later dubbed "the Crystal Palace." Disregarding the boys' contribution, Lambert took all the credit for the discovery for himself, and the youthful explorers have been forgotten over the years. Later cave owners kept tunneling and expanding, right up to today. Now it is one of the most highly rated caves in the Southeast by spelunkers (cave enthusiasts) because of its excellent condition and unique features.

Willie Cowan began working at Raccoon Mountain Caverns as a night guard and maintenance man in March 1966 and unofficially rejoined the staff as a ghost about nine months later after his gruesome death. And while caves are wondrous and creepy places, full of dangers that have killed many a person, Willie chose to enter the afterlife through the gift shop instead.

The bearded watchman, who was fond of worn flannel shirts, was friendly and well liked. His job included walking a regular beat through the cavern and guarding the gift shop after hours. He would often whistle while pacing through the cave. In between his rounds, he enjoyed relaxing with a cigar or pipe as he kept watch.

On November 30, 1966, Willie fell asleep in the gift shop, cigar in hand. A fire broke out, which not only burned Willie to a blackened crisp but also destroyed the gift shop, main building, and sky ride power plant. While rumors abounded of mysterious goings-on after Willie's death, it was not until the Perlaky family acquired the cave in the late 1990s that anyone was brave enough to speak about it.

Patty Perlaky says she first experienced the specter herself in 1995. But she had spoken to a man whose father had been the manager in the late 1960s and 1970s, and after Willie's death, he had heard footsteps in the cave when no one else was there.

Patty began keeping a diary of all the reported sights, sounds, and smells in the cavern caused by either an invisible source or an apparition that disappeared. She documented that many guests and guides smelled pipe or cigar smoke in the cavern, often in late November, as the anniversary date of the fateful fire approached. The smell usually occurred near the reflection pool and the stalagmite called "Iguana Head," as well as in the "Hall of Dreams." What could be causing a smell like that, far from the surface, where no smoking was allowed? People started whispering that it was the ghost of Willie, the beloved night watchman.

Patty, who had not been around in Willie's day, began doing her own research to find what might be haunting their cave. She found newspaper articles and reports about the fire and interviewed people about the night guard who was killed. She came to her own conclusion that it was indeed Willie, still on guard.

Sometimes cave explorers smell stinky carbide head lamps. The head lamps had been used back during Willie's time at the cave, but they hadn't been used in decades. Many employees working late at night in the gift shop heard footsteps on the stairs above when no one else was there.

Some guests and employees even saw a bearded man in ragged clothes vanish right before their eyes! Erin H., a guide at the park, looked up when she heard whistling near low-hanging Headache Rock at the front of the cave and saw this figure vanish right before her. Unlike the rest of us, Willie no longer has to worry about bumping his head. He can just pass right through the rock.

On a few occasions, Willie has gone a step farther to actually interact with guests. A guide was in the gift shop one day when she heard the sign rattle against the cave door. It was as if someone was shaking the doorknob, though no one was in the cave. When she called out, "Willie, stop it," the door mysteriously opened. In 1999, one of the owners, Bob Perlaky, chased a strange man in a red flannel shirt through the cave back to the main entrance, where the man simply disappeared. There was no place along the way any living person could have slipped away. Upon hearing her brother's story, Patty filled him in on the cavern's permanent guest. About a year later, Bob was speaking with some guests after the cave had been closed up for

the night when they heard the cave door slam. They then saw the light of a motion sensor go off under the door, inside the cave. They hurried in to give chase. Bob ran one way and the group of guests ran the other way to trap the intruder. However, neither group passed anyone before they met up in front of the cave entrance.

Several people have seen a small round floating blue light in the deepest parts of the cave. In fact, I saw this mysterious light with my own eyes! In January 2011, I was with a group who all spotted the glowing orb, despite the fact we were two hundred feet underground. Normally, overhead lights are kept on in the cave, but on this occasion, we were able to explore some areas using just flashlights. Someone suggested we all turn the flashlights off in one section. I have never before been in such total darkness. Suddenly, I saw a glowing light behind one girl's shoulder. When I asked who had turned their flashlight on, everyone was puzzled—until they saw it too! All, that is, except the girl it was floating behind. Suddenly she screamed. She said someone—or something—had grabbed her. And she pointed to the shoulder where the rest of us had seen the light! Wouldn't you scream if you were touched by a ghost?

So that no one is scared off, the cave guides do not talk about the haunting on the tour unless they are asked to. And if you are lucky enough to visit, ask them about Willie. If you are really lucky, you may even get a chance to experience him first hand. He is still there, looking after "his" guests.

Hales Bar Horrors

Hales Bar, a dam on the Tennessee River to the west of Chattanooga, is not only haunted—it is actually cursed!

In 1775, when the Cherokee were pressured to sign over their land in Tennessee and Kentucky, an angry Native American leader named Dragging Canoe said it was a bloody land and cursed it. That curse came back to haunt the builders and owners of Hales Bar more than a century later.

The people who built the dam thought they built it on solid rock. However, they had actually built it on limestone, which was filled with as many holes as Swiss cheese! It leaked from the moment they finished it in November 1913. They hired men called "the Rag Gang" to stuff the holes with cloth, but it did no good. Thousands of gallons of water per SECOND were bursting through the holes. In 1939, the TVA (Tennessee Valley Authority) thought they could fix it, but they finally gave up and blew up the dam and lock in 1968. They left the powerhouse, but it has been sinking more and more every year. Almost all the floors are underwater.

There is a "suck," or whirlpool, near the powerhouse, and superstitious folks say the souls of people who lost their lives in the river are trapped there. Some people even claim they've seen faces in the suck!

There are not only ghosts in the water—ghosts also haunt the entire building. A ghost

named Rachel occupies the upstairs. She has been recorded saying things like "Don't leave," and "I told you a secret." Near the steps, which now descend into the water, is a man in old-fashioned clothes who likes to stalk tour groups. He has been seen by several people, including a local radio personality who thought he was just seeing someone in a costume— until he disappeared! A ghost hunter later sent him a photo of a ghost from that location. Can you imagine his surprise when he saw it was

the same man? And a ghost hunter from a TV show caught a thermal image of the stalking shadow man.

There are railroad tracks going nowhere inside the building, left over from the days when the dam was operating. Even though the train has been gone for decades, a ghost whistle is still sometimes heard there.

The ghost of a young girl plays in the remains of a tunnel that previously ran under the river. Before the dam was destroyed, children once used the tunnel to get to the school on the other side. When I took my son to "her" tunnel, a ghost hunting app on my phone said, "Play." My son wouldn't ask her questions, but out of the blue he said, "Her mother and father are coming." That gave me chills! People have left her stuffed animals, toys, and candy. Even though no living person has been there in the meantime, the stuffed animals and toys disappear between visits by ghost hunters. However, the candy is left behind.

Another ghost haunts a cemetery on the grounds. When I was standing next to the haunted grave, my phone started dialing numbers on its own. Maybe it was Barney, the man whose grave it was, trying to use a cell phone to communicate with the living!

On April 24, 2010, a resolution was presented to and accepted by Cherokee leaders in Oklahoma to release the land from the ancient curse spoken by Dragging Canoe more than two centuries before. Perhaps he, the land, and the ghosts that haunt the place can rest in peace.

Haunted Hospital

You may have watched movies, TV shows, and YouTube videos about ghost hunting, and it usually looks adventurous, interesting, and even fun. But ghost hunting in real life is so much more than that—and a visit to Old South Pittsburg Hospital proved that.

Old South Pittsburg Hospital is an abandoned hospital just south of Chattanooga. The hospital opened its doors to the community in 1959 and closed its doors for good less than forty years later in 1998. The massive building sits on a lonely hill, and it is one of the most haunted hospitals in Tennessee. Like all hospitals, many of have died there. However, there is something that lingers there that feels older than the hospital itself.

The interior is a labyrinth of rooms that seem to have been frozen in time. Hospital beds still sit in rooms, and the nursing home at one end is still filled with the belongings of the last people to die there. And it is full of strange things no one expects to see in a hospital. There are piles of tires and old clothes. It smells musty, and the air is heavy with dust. When I first walked in, I was overwhelmed by the smell of mold and a feeling that something old was watching me. It felt wrong to be there, like I was walking on someone's grave.

Ghost-hunting teams go to the hospital all the time. For a small fee, the hospital is theirs for the night. These ghost hunters are never disappointed by the old hospital. Evidence of ghosts is as thick as the dust that covers the floors. I was lucky enough to get to explore Old South Pittsburg Hospital with the team from Southern Ghosts.

The team explained ghost hunting to me as they did their work. They set up dozens of cameras and motion detectors in rooms. They put toys in random places in the halls. They explained that they would later track the motion of these objects to keep tabs on the movements of the ghosts. It took over an hour for the team to set up all their equipment, and then we got ready for the ghosts to show up.

The team used EMF detectors and a medium to do their first rounds through the hospital.

An EMF detector is an electromagnetic field detector, and most ghost hunters believe that ghosts and spirits cause spikes in the electromagnetic field. So when an EMF detector reads spikes, it means a ghost is near.

The medium used her unique ability to communicate with ghosts to sense which rooms were the most active. The team members followed behind her with their EMF detectors and thermometers. Using these tools, we picked rooms to sit in and talk to the dead.

Talking to the dead isn't as exciting as it sounds. Ghost hunters use voice recorders to record EVP, or electronic voice phenomena. We sat in the room for hours asking questions to empty space, hoping to capture EVP on a recorder. We asked questions like, "Is anyone there?" "Is there anything can we do for you?" and "Why are you still here?" and we waited and listened to silence. After an hour or so of this, my mind started to wander, and I started fidgeting with my zipper and got up and walked away.

The next night, the team played the EVP back for me. We heard a voice on the recording say, "The old lady likes you," and then heard the sound of me playing with my zipper. It was the creepiest thing I had ever heard. I had been sitting right there playing with my zipper, in an otherwise completely silent room. But the recording on the EVP proved that the ghost of someone was there and had spoken.

Southern Ghosts was not the only team to catch this kind of phenomena at the hospital. Other teams have caught images of people standing in the psychiatric ward, and others have caught an old man sitting on one of the beds. There is video of the toys left out by the team moving on their own, and the EVP recorders are filled with the voices that only answer when everything is quiet.

We don't know who these ghosts at Old South Pittsburg Hospital are, but it's very clear that they still like to have visitors . . .

Supernatural Creatures

Not all of Chattanooga's spooky tales involve ghosts. At least two strange and mysterious creatures have been spotted around the city: one large and scary-looking, but actually rather playful, and the other child-sized, but downright terrifying!

Creatures whose existence is disputed have been reported all over the world, and the search for and study of these elusive beasts is called cryptozoology. They include the Loch Ness monster and its North American cousins Ogopogo and Champy, the Moth Man, Yeti, and Bigfoot (who has been spotted near Chattanooga and known locally as "the Wild Man"). These strange beings that tease us by appearing only briefly are rumored to live in many states—including Tennessee.

You've heard of Scotland's Loch Ness monster, or Nessie, as she is known, right? But did you know that at one time, Chattanooga was home to such a creature? That's right!

According to many people, the Tennessee River was home to a colossal water beast that hid in its murky depths. It surprised unsuspecting boaters by raising its fearsome head out of the water and steaming toward them at more than twenty miles per hour. Would you be frightened if something like that was heading straight for you? I would be!

Native Americans reported seeing the serpent as early as 1820. They knew to keep a watch out while drifting down the river and stay far away if they saw something large

moving under the water. The creature was also mentioned in several Chattanooga newspaper articles. According to one article that ran on July 2, 1885, this was not merely a giant fish. This monster was said to be twenty to twenty-five feet long, two feet wide, and had a head like a dog, with slime oozing from its skin and foam dripping from its gnashing teeth. The two-foot-high fin on its back stuck out of the water as it slithered along like a snake. One person who got dangerously close reported that it had a yellow belly and a blue back. It could even cross the wide river in just one minute! If THAT was not bad enough, when it was in a playful mood, it liked to tip over canoes, dumping the terrified paddlers into the drink with it. However, it was all in fun; it never so much as nibbled them. That did not make them any less scared, though!

The creature, let's call it "Phoenix," liked to hang out below the surface of the Tennessee River in an area of Chattanooga now known as Harrison. However, it would swim between there and another area of town called Dallas, which at that time was the county seat. It was not only reported to have been seen by the Native Americans; dozens of folks came forward, both kids and adults, including the very serious and stern father of a judge. It was whispered that many folks who saw it died mysteriously within a year. Yet the sightings became less frequent as more boats disturbed the waters. But who knows? The mysterious river monster may be lurking there still. Keep your eyes peeled if you go boating on the Tennessee River!

The more ominous creature was seen in the late 1980s or early 1990s at Memorial Park

Cemetery in Red Bank, more often called the Duck Pond Cemetery. There is a small building at the front of the graveyard, and near it stands an old oak tree. Guards hung out in the building in between their rounds. One night, while enjoying a little inside break, a guard who patrolled the cemetery grounds for more than twenty years heard something moving outside. As he went out to take a look, the rustling got louder. It sounded as if it was coming from the old oak tree. He lifted his flashlight, and what he saw there scared him so badly he raced back inside and locked the door. There in the branches was a strange creature. It had a face and arms and legs and was no more than three feet tall. But this was no child! It looked more like an alien or something you would see in a horror movie. For several minutes, the guard told himself his eyes must be playing tricks on him. Finally, he crept back outside and was at first relieved when he saw nothing in the tree. But then he heard a nearby noise and saw the creature crouching on the ground a few feet from him, snarling. He ran faster than he ever had in his life! The thing chased him all through the cemetery. The monster gave up its chase when the guard ran out into the street and reached his car.

The poor guard came back at daybreak to collect his things and quit. He refused to ever go back there for the rest of his life. I don't blame him, do you?!

Lookout Mountain

The Ghosts of Lookout Mountain

Lookout Mountain is one of my favorite places in Chattanooga. It sits high above the city and is home to beautiful trails, cool caves, and a splendid waterfall. I go there all the time to enjoy the natural beauty, but there is a dark side to this beautiful tourist attraction. The mountain is crawling with ghosts.

Noccalula Falls is the most stunning part of Lookout Mountain. It is so picturesque, but there is story about this beautiful waterfall that is one of the saddest on the mountain. It is the story of a Native American princess called Noccalula. Like most princesses, she was supposed to marry a man her father approved of. But the princess did not like her father's plans, and she had plans of her own. The princess had met a brave from another tribe, and the two fell madly in love. They could only hide their love for so long, and when they were discovered, Noccalula was forbidden from ever seeing her love again. The princess was heartbroken and wandered up to the top of the waterfall in utter sorrow. She threw herself off the top of the treacherous falls and fell to

her death. When her father learned of what happened, he was also heartbroken and named the waterfall after his beloved daughter. To this day, many people describe seeing the lovely Noccalula wandering along the top of the waterfall, forever mourning her lost love.

But Noccalula is not alone in haunting the mountain. In November 1863, in the Battle of Lookout Mountain, or the Battle Above the Clouds, Union forces took the mountain from Confederate forces. It was a brutal battle. Many soldiers fought in hand-to-hand combat, and over 1,600 soldiers died that day above the cloud. But one group of Union soldiers got lost in the mountains and wandered for days. Over time, locals and nature picked off the poor men. Those that know the mountain tell stories of how the lost soldiers still roam trying to find their way home.

Some of the scariest ghosts on Lookout Mountain haunt the caves around Ruby Falls. Their story starts with a cave explorer named Mr. Lomax. Lomax was mapping the cave systems around Ruby Falls and was deep underground when his light failed. Lomax was trapped in utter darkness and had no idea how to find his way out. A search party was sent to find him, and when he was found, every hair on his head had turned white, and he was too terrified to speak of what had happened to him in the caves. Lomax left the area, never to return, but when further exploration of the cave was completed, old bones were found in the cavern. Locals say the icy fingers of the ghosts who left their bones behind had gripped Lomax in the dark and drove him insane. They say that parts of the cave are haunted and that those who venture too far will meet the ghosts that turned Lomax's hair white.

There are many ghosts on Lookout Mountain. They are so numerous that if you wander around the mountain, you are bound to trip over one eventually . . .

CHAPTER 11

Look Out for
Valley Ghouls!

The towns of Lookout Valley and St. Elmo, which are tucked into the foot of Lookout Mountain, host several ghosts. I was lucky enough to have heard one of them! (If you consider hearing a ghost lucky.)

St. Elmo is now an artsy subdivision of the city, but in the old days, it was the "Wild West" of Chattanooga. There were bars, saloons, racetracks, and other places where people went to have a good time. Which also meant there was gambling, fights, duels, and general mischief. St. Elmo also had some really funny laws. The town banned kite flying, dressing like the opposite sex, throwing missiles, and slingshots. It did, however, allow skinny-dipping, but only in certain places.

St. Elmo has two cemeteries. The larger of the two, Forest Hills, has a famous gravestone. Captain William R. Frye, one of the city's most prominent and well-liked citizens, died in 1910. He has a marker that says, "I came here without being consulted and leave without my consent." The ghosts there also do not want to leave. In a small back area of Forest Hills, there is a very old children's section, and the cries of babies have often been heard there. Children have been spotted among those graves, only to disappear right before the eyes of onlookers. There is also the classic "woman in white" ghost who wanders around. A member of the ghost hunting group Paranormal Researchers Of the South East (PROSE) has seen her weeping there twice, and both times, she disappeared in a flash of white. There is also a tall black shadow form that strolls through the grounds. He floats from the back of a nearby grocery store to the burial ground.

But St. Elmo is also home to a small, dark, creepy abandoned graveyard that very few people know about. Thurman Cemetery is tucked back in the woods near a garbage dump and is overgrown with trees, briars, and underbrush. There are some very fancy tombstones, but there are also several graves marked simply by small blank stones. Those are thought to be the final resting place of enslaved people. The legend is that if you visit late at night, you will see them there. A ghost soldier has also been seen heading there from a nearby historic home. The founder of St. Elmo, Colonel A.M. Johnson, had a house near that site that burned down. Maybe it is his ghost, still wandering through town. While he is supposedly a friendly ghost, I'm not sure I want to take the chance and approach him. Would you?

A very different ghost haunts another historic location in Lookout Valley. Brown's Ferry Tavern is a log cabin on the Trail of Tears. The Trail of Tears, which took place in the 1830s, was the forced march of many Native

Americans from their homes in Tennessee and other states to Oklahoma. Many people died on the way. In 1838, one of the places the displaced people were held before beginning their march was this cabin. The cabin and nearby ferry were formerly owned by John Brown from 1803 until he himself was forced on the Trail of Tears. Brown had a reputation as a very friendly host, but he was also thought to be a serial killer.

Many traders heading south to sell their goods would stop at Brown's Ferry Tavern for the night. John Brown was especially nice to those with the most goods to sell, so traders with their pockets full of gold would make sure to stop again on their way back home. He would put them in an upper bedroom far away from anyone else, where they could not be

heard. It is believed that in the middle of the night, John Brown would slip into the traders' room and murder them. After pocketing their money, he would take their body and wagon out on his ferry and dump them in the river. In the morning, John Brown would tell the other guests that the trader had run out in the middle of the night. People talked about what a good Christian man he was for not chasing the thieving trader for the money he owed! Little did they know . . .

The crimes were eventually discovered, but not until long after John Brown's death in 1847. More than one hundred years later, when the river was dredged in the area where the ferry had run, they found wagon hubs and human bones. A nearby historical marker doesn't name the killer, but it does say that several people were murdered at Brown's Ferry and Tavern.

The inn has been bought and sold several times over the years. It was often used as a private home, and there have been periods when it has lain dark and empty. Many people have reported seeing lights in the windows when there were no occupants. Some folks say they heard thuds like a body and chains being dragged. Bloodstains on the floor of the room where the unsuspecting traders were killed continue to reappear, despite scrubbing and even replacement of the wood. I saw them myself!

The home lay vacant after the death of the last owner, Joan Franks, in 2013. A developer who owned the property for a short time gave Chattanooga Ghost Tours permission to conduct ghost hunts in the tavern in 2016 and 2017. Some of John Brown's descendants, who acknowledged their ancestor was a murderer, joined the hunt.

During the very first investigation, in August 2016, a piece of equipment called an Ovilus answered "thirty-eight" when asked how many ghosts were there. (The Ovilus converts electromagnetic waves, believed to be created by ghosts, into words.) When I was telling the story to a newly arrived guide later that night, I had just said, "We asked how many spir-," when the Ovilus interrupted me again and said, "thirty-eight!" Do you think that might be the number of people John Brown killed there? I do. A ghostly figure also showed up that night on the SLS XCam. (SLS stands for "structured light sensor," and the camera captures the presence of ghosts on its screen.) This ghost even raised its right and then left hand when asked to do so! Later that month, we asked it to "kick" one of the guests who was showing up on the screen next to the spirit, and it did, several times. (Luckily, our guest felt nothing!)

I lived very close to the tavern when my kids were young. Ghosts often communicate more easily with children, maybe because they still have open minds. One day, my daughter Melody came running up the stairs, saying she had just heard a ghost say, "Hello, milady." I teased her, saying it was probably saying her name. Then I explained that we built the house,

no one else ever lived there, and certainly no one had ever died there. So there was no way it could be a ghost. Years later, when researching John Brown, I found out our neighborhood had been the site of a Civil War battle. Perhaps the ghost that greeted my daughter was a soldier with good manners . . .

Hunter Museum of American Art

The Haunting of Hunter Museum

The Hunter Museum sits on a bluff high above Chattanooga. Not only are the hundreds of paintings, photographs, sculptures, and decorative works of art lovely to look at, but the view from the bluff behind the museum is also stunning. And if you like murder mysteries and ghosts, you are sure to like the story of the oldest building that is part of the museum.

The museum is made up of three separate buildings. The oldest building, erected as a private home in 1904, came to be known as 15 Bluff View Drive. Locals called it "Bluff View Home." One day in 1925, the then owner of the home found a complete skeleton buried in the floor. Of course, she was terrified, and she immediately called the police. Joseph A. Paradiso was called in to investigate the case. He couldn't believe what he saw. The skeleton was dressed in women's clothing and wearing jewelry and glasses. And the skeleton had a very odd smell.

The bones were taken to the coroner, and he determined that the odd smell was ammonia. The coroner later testified in court that that was proof that the woman beneath the floor had been murdered. He said that her body was treated with ammonia to hide the smell of the decomposing body and that whoever had hidden the body in the basement was clearly trying to hide evidence of their horrible crime.

Neighbors, and anyone who knew the people who had lived there before, were interviewed. Some people remembered a family who had lived in the house from 1913 to 1917: Nancy Bennett, her son William, and Nancy's sister, Augusta Hoffman. They had seemed like a nice family. Augusta was liked, and the neighborhood children called her "Aunt Gus." In 1915, the neighbors recalled that Aunt Gus had suddenly disappeared. She went to the bank and took out all her money, and no one ever saw her again. The Bennetts moved out of the house shortly after that, saying that Augusta had run off with some man.

Investigator Paradiso thought this story sounded fishy, and he wanted to find out more about Nancy and William Bennett and Augusta Hoffman. The Bennetts weren't able to say who Augusta had run off with and where she now lived. Plus, the clothing and jewelry found on the skeleton belonged to Augusta. Investigator Paradiso was able to prove that the Bennetts had asked Augusta to move in and then took all her money and murdered her! In 1925, the Bennetts were convicted for Augusta's murder. It seemed like an open-and-shut case.

In 1970, Bluff View Home was torn down to make way for a museum expansion. Shortly after that, employees of the Hunter Museum began noticing a woman wandering the halls admiring the artwork after the museum was closed. It obviously wasn't a museum visitor, because this woman disappeared right before their eyes. Those who work there believe it is poor Augusta Hoffman, forever trapped where she was betrayed and buried. But at least she has beautiful things to look at in the afterlife . . .

The stories we have chosen to share have hopefully given you an idea of Chattanooga's fascinating history, as well as its eerie legends, ghastly ghosts, and spooky spirits. We hope you get a chance to explore and discover this beautiful city—and we also hope you get to meet some of the things that lurk in the shadows and go bump in the night while you're in Chattanooga.

Amy Petulla practiced law for twenty years- until she left it for a job that was much more fun. In 2007, she founded Chattanooga Ghost Tours, Inc, now one of the top ten ghost tours in the nation. Amy hopes that this adaptation of her first book, *Haunted Chattanooga,* will leave young readers with the same love of books that she has enjoyed her whole life.

Jessica Penot is a writer and therapist who lives in Northern Alabama. Jessica is the author of seven novels, including the middle grade fantasy book, *The Monster Hunter's Manual.* Jessica loves ghost stories and things that go bump in the night, and you can find her wandering haunted places all over the world in her spare time. You can learn more about her at www.jessicapenot.net and at www.treeolifebehavioral.com.

Check out some of the other Spooky America titles available now!

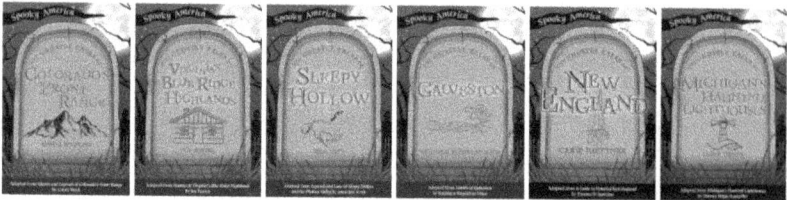

Spooky America was adapted from the creeptastic Haunted America series for adults. Haunted America explores historical haunts in cities and regions across America. Each book chronicles both the widely known and less-familiar history behind local ghosts and other unexplained mysteries. Here's more from *Haunted Chattanooga* authors Amy Petulla and Jessica Penot :

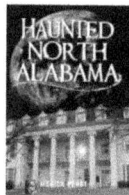

Learn more about Chattanooga Ghost Tours at
ChattanoogaGhostTours.com